Little Voices
Ballads

NOVELLO PUBLISHING LIMITED
part of The Music Sales Group
London / New York / Paris / Sydney / Copenhagen / Berlin / Madrid / Hong Kong / Tokyo

Published by
Novello Publishing Limited
14-15 Berners Street, London, W1T 3LJ, UK.

Exclusive distributors:
Music Sales Limited
Distribution Centre, Newmarket Road,
Bury St Edmunds, Suffolk, IP33 3YB, UK.

Music Sales Pty Limited
Units 3-4, 17 Willfox Street, Condell Park
NSW 2200, Australia.

Arranged by Barrie Carson Turner.
Edited by Rachel Payne.
Music processed by Paul Ewers Music Design.

Printed in the EU.

www.musicsales.com

Angels

Words & Music by
Robbie Williams & Guy Chambers

the pla - ces where we go when we're grey and old?___

Pla - ces where we go when we're grey and old?___

F   Bb

'Cause I've been___ told that sal - va - tion let's their wings___

That sal - va - tion let's their wings___

C   Gm7   Bb

_un - fold;___ So when I'm ly - ing in my bed, thoughts

_un - fold;___ So when I'm ly - ing in my bed, thoughts

run - ning through my head. and I feel that love is dead,___

run - ning through my head. and I feel that love is dead,___

I'm lov-ing an-gels in-stead.___ And through it all___

I'm lov-ing an-gels in-stead.___

Eb   Bb/D   Bb   F/A   C

___ she of-fers me___ pro-tec - tion, a lot of love and af-fec-

She of-fers me___ pro-tec - tion, lot of love and af-fec-

G/B   G   Am

7

tion   whe-ther I'm right   or   wrong.   And down the wa - ter - fall___

tion   whe-ther I'm right   or   wrong.

F   C

___   wher-ev - er it___ may take   me,   I know that life___ won't break

Wher - ev - er it___ may take   me,   know that life___ won't break

G/B   G   Am

me; when I come to call_____ She won't for-sake_____ me,

me; when I come to call_____ For-sake me,_____

I'm lov-ing an-gels in-stead._____ And through it all_____

_____ I'm lov-ing an-gels in-stead._____

Can You Feel The Love Tonight

Words by Tim Rice
Music by Elton John

when the heat___ of the roll-ing world___ can be turned___ a-way.___
that the twist-ing ka-lei-do-scope___ moves us all_____ in turn.___

when the heat___ of the roll-ing world___ can be turned___ a-way.___
that the twist-ing ka-lei-do-scope___ moves us all_____ in turn.___

Db   Ab/C   Ab   Bbm   Eb/G

An en-chant-ed mo - ment,   and it sees___ me through.___
There's a rhyme and rea - son   to the wild___ out - doors,_____

An en-chant-ed mo - ment,   and it sees___ me through.___
There's a rhyme and rea - son   to the wild___ out - doors,_____

Db   Ab/C   Db   Ab/C

It's e-nough_ for this rest-less war-ri-or just to be_ with you._ And
when the heart_ of this star-crossed voy-a-ger beats in time_ with yours._

It's e-nough_ just to be_ with you._
when the heart_ beats in time_ with yours._

Db Fm Gb Eb

can you feel the love_ to-night? It is where we are._
can you feel the love_ to-night, how it's laid to rest?

And can you feel the love?_ It is where we are,_
And can you feel the love?_ how it's laid to rest,_

Ab Eb/G Fm Db Ab Db Bb/D

It's e - nough_____ for this
It's e - nough_____ to make

we are.
to rest.

for this
to make

Eb   Db   Ab/C

1.

wide_ eyed_ wan-der-er   that we got this far._____   And

wide_ eyed_ wan-der-er   that we got this far,_____   this far.

Fm   Db   Bbm Ab/C Db Bb/D   Eb

13

2. **To Coda ⊕**

kings_ and_ va-ga-bonds_ be-lieve the ve - ry best._

kings_ and_ va-ga-bonds_ be-lieve the ve - ry best._

⊕ **Coda**

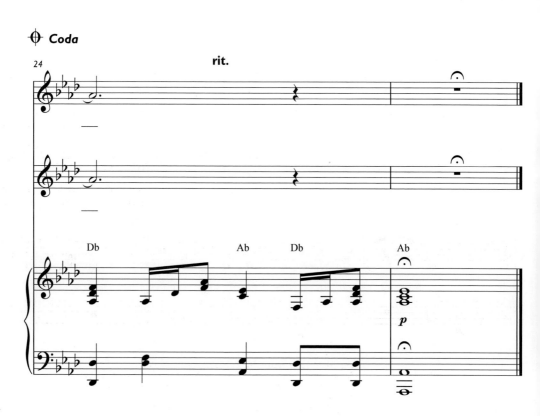

rit.

Dear Jessie

Words & Music by
Madonna Ciccone & Pat Leonard

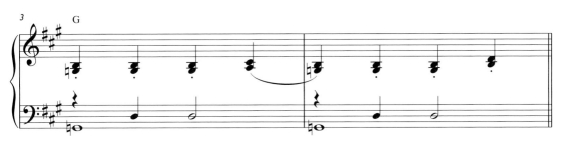

Ba - by face don't grow so fast,__ make__ spe - cial wish__ that will

make be - lieve__ is in - side your heart__ it will

al - ways last. Rub this ma - gic lan - tern, he will make your
nev - er leave. There's a gold - en gate where the fair - ies all wait and

al - ways last. Rub this ma - gic lan - tern, he will make your
nev - er leave. There's a gold - en gate where the fair - ies all wait and

E   A   E/G#   F#m7   C#m/E

dreams come true___   for you.___   1. Ride the   rain-bow to the
danc - ing moons,   for you.___   2. Close your   eyes___ and___

dreams come true___   for you.___   1. Ride the   rain-bow to the
danc - ing moons,   for you.___   2. Close your   eyes___ and___

D   E/D A/C# E7/B   D

16

oth - er side._ Catch a fall - ing star_ and then take a ride to the
you'll be there,_ where the mer - maids sing_ as they comb their hair. Like a

oth - er side._ Catch a fall - ing star_ and then take a ride to the
you'll be there,_ where the mer - maids sing_ as they comb their hair. Like a

C#m   F#m   E

riv - er that sings and the clo-ver that brings good luck to you,_ it's all true._
foun - tain of gold you can nev-er grow old where dreams are made,_ your love pa - rade.

riv - er that sings and the clo-ver that brings good luck to you,_ it's all true._
foun - tain of gold you can nev-er grow old where dreams are made,_ your love pa - rade.

A   E/G#   F#m7   C#m/E   D   Bm7   E7

Pink e - le-phants and le - mon- ade, dear___ Jes - sie, hear the laugh - ter

Pink e - le-phants and le - mon- ade, hear the laugh - ter

run - ning through__ the love par - ade. Can - dy kiss - es and a sun - ny day, dear___

through__ the love par - ade. Can - dy kiss - es and a sun - ny day,

Jes - sie see the ros - es rain - ing on___ the love pa - rade. If the land of

see the ros - es on___ the love pa - rade. If the land of

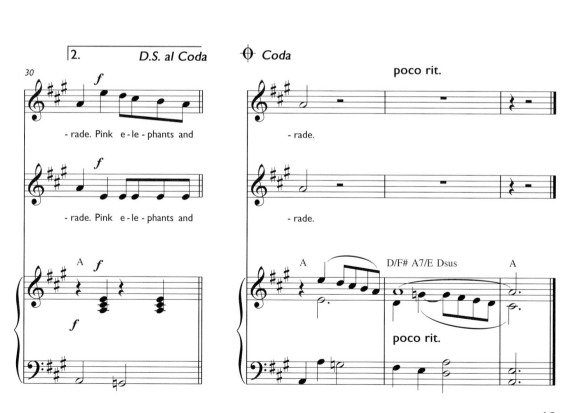

- rade. Pink e - le - phants and

- rade. Pink e - le - phants and

- rade.

- rade.

When You Believe

Words & Music by Stephen Schwartz

Ma-ny nights we've prayed, with
In this time of fear, when

Ma-ny nights we've prayed, with
In this time of fear, when

no proof a-ny-one could hear. In our hearts a hope-ful song__ we
prayer so of-ten proves in vain, hope seems like the sum-mer birds,__ too

no proof a-ny-one could hear. A hope-ful song,
prayer so of-ten proves in vain, the sum-mer birds,

bare - ly un - der - stood. Now we are not a - fraid, al -
swift - ly flown a - way. Yet now I'm stand - ing here, my

bare - ly un - der stood._ We are not a - fraid,
swift - ly flown a - way._ Now I'm stand - ing here,

Am7　　　　Bsus　　Bm　　E　　　D

though we know there's much to fear. We were mov - ing moun - tains long__ be -
heart so full I can't ex - plain, seek - ing faith and speak - ing words_ I

there's much to fear. We were mov - ing moun - tains
I can't ex - plain, seek - ing faith and speak - ing

Bm7　　　　Em　　　　C　　　　G/B

rit.

When you be-lieve, some-how you will. You will when you__ be-

lieve, some - how you will. When you be -

Em   Bm7   C   G/B   Am7 G/B   C   D7

1.
a tempo

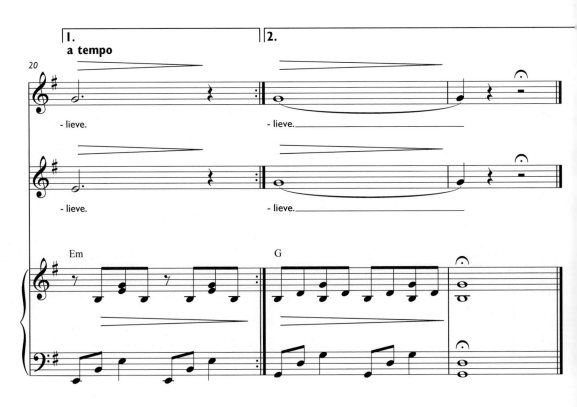

- lieve.

- lieve.

2.

- lieve._____

- lieve._____

Em   G

24

You Raise Me Up

Words & Music by
Rolf Lovland & Brendan Graham

come_____ and my__ heart bur-dened be, then I am

when trou-bles come, heart bur-dened be,_____

Eb/G   Ab   Bbsus   Bb

still_____ and wait__ here__ in the si - lence, un - til you__

I am still__ and wait__ here__ in the si - lence,

Ab   Eb   Ab

come and sit a while_ with_ me._____ You raise me

'til you come_ and sit a while_ with me._____ You raise me

Eb/Bb   Bb7sus   Eb   Cm/Eb G7/D

up so I can stand on moun-tains. You raise_ me up to walk on storm-y

up so I can stand on moun-tains. You raise me up to walk on storm-y

Cm   Ab   Eb/G   G7   Cm   Ab

up to more than I can be.

decresc.

Raise me up to more than I can be.

F/C   Csus   C7   F

rit.

pp